Scattered to the Wind

Leo R. Hunt

ABOUT THE COVER

The Cover asks a question.

There are three leaves on the cover and three words.
                Life   Love   Hope
Two of the leaves are blown in the wind.
There is one leaf still clinging to the tree.
The question is what name would you put on the Leaf still clinging to the tree?

Scattered to the Wind
Copyright © 2022 by Leo R. Hunt

All rights reserved. No part of this publication may be reproduced, distributed, or transmitted in any form or by any means, including photocopying, recording, or other electronic or mechanical methods, without the prior written permission of the publisher or author, except in the case of brief quotations embodied in critical reviews and certain other noncommercial uses permitted by copyright law.

ISBN: (Paperback)   978-1-63945-440-2
         (eBook)   978-1-63945-441-9

Writers' Branding Revised Date: 12/12/2022

The view expressed in this book are solely those of the author and do not necessarily reflect the views of the publisher, and the publisher hereby disclaims any responsibility for them.

Writers' Branding
1-800-608-6550
www.writersbranding.com
orders@writersbranding.com

CONTENTS

About the cover ii
Acknowledgment xi

Be kind to me 1
It takes 2
Unfulfilled 3
Freedom 4
My Mind 5
How sweet 7
Life is 8
The Fire Within Me 9
What is 10
It is I Father 11
Before 13
The Silent 14
Life's Truth 15
A shadow in your mind 16
Sing 17
Love spoke to me 18
Are you living? 19
Sing 20
Some one 21
Walk-In A Dream 22
Another Day 23
It Will Take 24
Yesterday, Word 25
I Have lived 27

I Wander	28
It May	29
We've	30
A Pennys worth of sleep	31
I Have Lived	32
Why Do I	33
Been at War	34
I Have Enjoyed	35
The Future	36
Hand	38
Summer night	39
Listen	40
Success	41
Words No Longer	42
The melody	43
The Tree/Your Yesterday/I Don't	44
Dissident	45
Good By	46
I Call Out	47
No Longer	48
Love/Beauty/When	49
Love was young	50
I am not	51
Hallelujah	52
Blackest night	53
Tomorrow	54
Given Life	55
Oh	56
I have nothing	57
Holy	58
When I was young	59
The Wind	60
Midnight moon	60
Because	61

Tomorrow/For Life/Peace	63
A White Horse	64
They	65
I Wonder	66
The Festival of not Returning	67
Children of Greed	68
Like I am	69
I Know/The Sun/Someone	70
I am	71
Love spoke to Me	73
How Sweet	74
If I were young	75
Before Today	76
I Have Come	77
I Forecast	78
My Past	79
Man Is	80
How Do You	81
The Words	82
My Voice	83
Good Morning Life	84
I Am	85
More	86
I Know	87
The voice of the Mountain	88
For Sheep	89
Words	90
I Look	91
As Far	92
Yesterday	93
Tomorrow called	94
I Was a storm	95
I Have Song	96
Tomorrows Dream	97

Letter to a Dream	98
Four Strokes to Midnight	99
A Top	101
I Am firm	102
Love is	103
I Have walked	104
One Thing	105
Sing Oh Heart	106
There is	107
Acknowledge	109
Today	110
They Say/ If You	111
Was It the Master?	112
It's come up again	113
Walk in Life	114
Ask	115
Silent	116
Have	117
The Wind	118
More Than / I was never	119
I no longer	120
I am Here	121
Yesterday	122
In All	124
With Love	125
To My Father 1984	126
I Awoke	127
I'll Cry/Life is/Love hate	128
I Have been Listening	129
Happiness/I Spend/It Is/Some	130
The Breath	131
Acid Rain	132
At the End	134

*I dedicate this book to my wife
and our families*

Give a voice to the one you love,

But not to drown out the passion

ACKNOWLEDGMENT

I have to acknowledge my Lord Jesus Christ for the words and the ability to put them on paper, because of my struggle to spell the word and my dyslexia, it was a miracle that any of my words ever appeared on a paper.

I also thank Him for giving my wife the patience and the love to withstand the lonely hours it took me to put the first book and this book together.

My confession and apology lie in two of my poems, "Blown in the Wind" and "I Never Had a Dream".

Tomorrow is not just another day.

It is a day more precious than Gold.

A special thanks to my editor, Janene Hunt

Tech support
Gotcha Secretarial Services,
www.gotchasecretarial.com

BE KIND TO ME

Yesterday's voices haunts me
    it whispers of
    love, joy, and
    pain.I will not
    give into
    what
        I cannot see
            To Tomorrow
                Tomorrow be kind to me.

*

IT TAKES

It takes longer to
    break a habit
Then to make a habit

UNFULFILLED

It seems I must do something I have
not done. Somewhere I must go
that I have never been.
I have a feeling I cannot dismiss,
a feeling that I have reached for
but cannot grasp.
A dream I have not fulfilled.
There are words I have not spoken.
Words I have not heard or dream of
what I may become or how I may
understand who I am.
I seek to know who I was and what I will become.
For the answers do I look to the future
or to the past or do I just live this life as
 long as it last.

FREEDOM

You have killed the lamb of freedom; it lies
bleeding on the ground. You have stolen
our peace that we wore like a crown.
Have we lost the light of freedom?
Is it all back and doom or is the
son of freedom hidden in a darken room?
Can you hear freedom song? The one that
all free people sing.
Can you hear freedom song?
Can you hear the joy it brings?
The ones that fought for freedom now lie
in their graves, their lives have been for
gotten and for them freedom rings.
Oh, people that are near tomorrow have come and
if you sing freedom song surely it will be near.
We must save our freedom for all the young that
are here. We must keep our freedom and show
the young we care, so they will not have to go
to war and k i l l.

MY MIND

My mind, My Heart,
What of these things within me?
My Life? My death? What of these
  things that I await. My yesterday's,
  my past. What is life? What of me?
  Why do I give it away, to know that
  once it was mine.
Why must I take to know I do not Want.
Will there be peace in life,
  or must I wait until eternity?

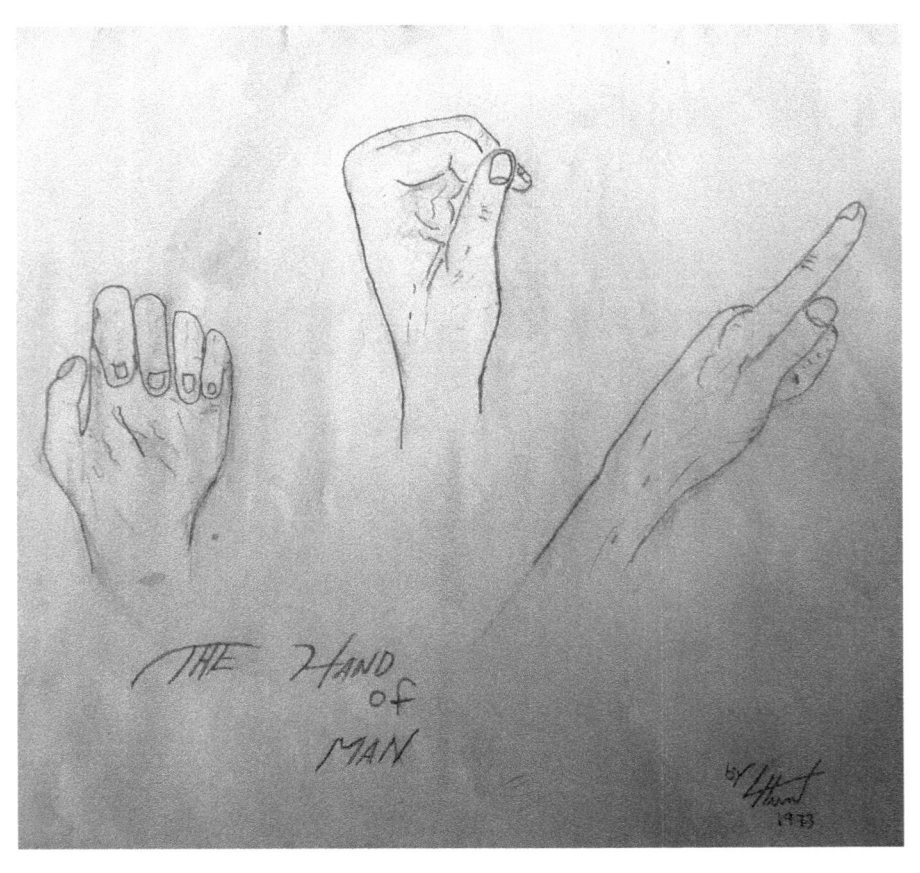

"THE HAND OF MAN"

HOW SWEET

How sweet old age
I just wish you didn't have to die from it.

*

Love is like a tender flower
You must protect it from the weeds,
you are the Gardener.

LIFE IS

Life is like a flower in the gardener.
It needs equal

parts of rain and sunshine.

THE FIRE WITHIN ME

The fire that burned within me is much
dimmer now. The dream of the future and its
happening seems much slimmer now.

I still have the desire to do the thing I did before,
but the drive source is much smaller now.

The dream of tomorrow is still within me,
but the brightness Is much darker now.

My tomorrows call my name much softer now.

I spend my time wondering where the
time has gone, and a life left behind.

I do not despair that time has gone so quickly
nor do I cry over the moments lost, but now
I give thanks for the moments gained.

WHAT IS

What is the voice of man but a whisper?
What is the life of man, But a moment?
What meaning can man bring to the earth? His truth.
His love. His understanding, What of his Gods?
If man were not, would the earth be?
What of his words, does he speak
forever after?

Does his voice cry in the wildness?
Is he here just to be the earth custodian?
If man is to live on this earth
must he prove his worth or
live and die without
revealing his truth?

IT IS I FATHER

It is I, father, your son, back from a war
we fought. We fought and won,
we fought and died. It is I, father, your son,
back from a war hundred years older but
what I have seen. You, father, who have
not been to war, cannot see the hell war
brings. If only there were a way to tear
from my mind all the man-made terrors
of death. If only I could close my eyes
and not see the blood of my fellowman
flowing on the ground. If only I could
close my ears to the screams of pain and
the fear of death that war has engraved
there, the echo of voices calling in the
black hell of men dying alone.

Old men crying for their mothers as if lost
from them. Let me live all that I will.
Pray for the young that they do not
have to go to war and kill.

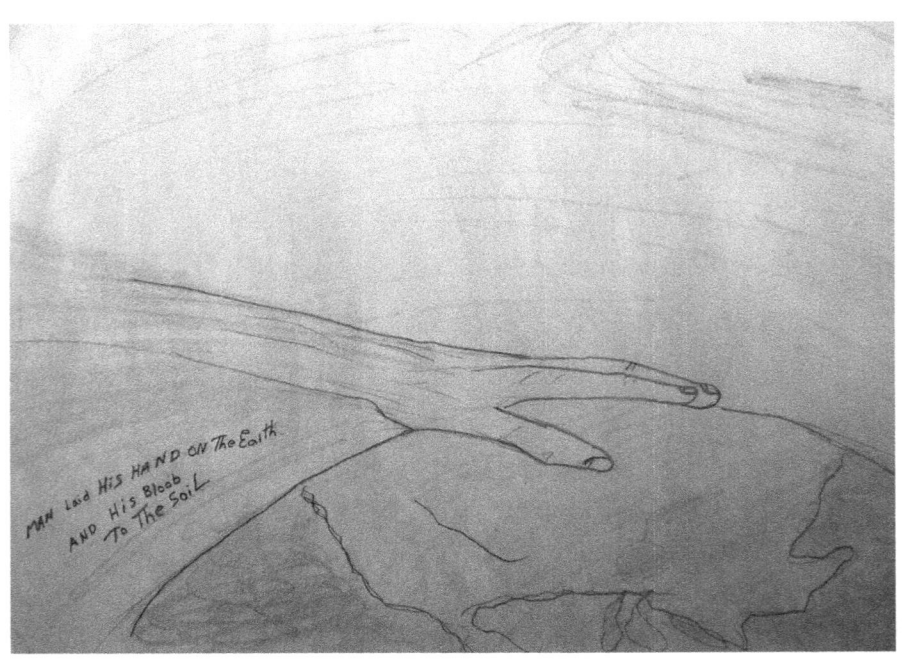

MAN LAID HIS HAND ON THE EARTH AND HIS BLOOD TO SOIL

BEFORE

Before the sun has been covered by the
worst of man and its rays devoured by his dust.

Let the blossom of the rose show its glory
once more. Before the rain from the sky
brought life and sweetness to the earth,
Now it seems to take your breath away.
Love and happiness flew on the wings of a
dove and life moved in rhythm to time.
Then the footstep of man covers the roses.

Today the earth is on the doorstep of
man's evolution, to another life.
And there will be no more roses.

THE SILENT

The silent passing of time
beckons me to its serenity.
The wilderness await.
The quiet times reaches
into man's soul.
Take time to watch the trees
grow, to watch the clouds
on high. Breathe deeply the
air, taste its freshness.
Now is the time to feel and
reason the day. Take unto
you the peace that is within
your heart and fill your cup.

When you are at peace, the thunder
will soften and the rain will feel
like a kiss from your God.

LIFE'S TRUTH

I walk on the path of life looking for the truth,
the truth that has been hidden from
me by my own blindness.

It was like looking into a dark pit and I was
staring into the asses looking for the light.

I walked among men not seeing their pain,
just things that would bring me beauty
and things that would bring me wealth.

The years numbered greatly and
in my higher years the light began
to shine, and I was awakened.

The light became brighter and melted
away the mist that covered me and I have
been set adrift on the sea of reality and
I am carried on the tide of humanity.

A SHADOW IN YOUR MIND

I know I am just a shadow in
your mind a love left behind.
A hidden melody, a long last tear.
A kiss that still burns on your lips.
Your heart skips a beat as
a passing dream fades. A
dream that now grows cold
A love you no longer hold.
A goodbye that still rings
in your ears. A goodbye
that still brings a tear.
But these days are gone and you
have moved on. When you speak
of love that you had long ago, I
am still a shadow in your mind.

SING

I have sung now my sorrows, they have gone
from me, and they fly on wings of happiness.
I have a song to sing that will make you cry tears of
joy. For he that has never lived in life, let him live now.
Let him find the words in his heart that
may carry him from life to living.

LOVE SPOKE TO ME

Love came to me and said, "Tell me who I am".
I thought for a time and before I spoke, I turned
away. "Love" I began, you are a dream, you
are a thought, you are a feeling, a fantasy."

I stopped and turned to Love but Love had turned
away I tried to say more but the words were frozen
to my lips. Then Love's words came from the mist,
"Until you know my truth, I will walk from you".
I cried out, "I do know your truth". "Love", I began,
"You're what all people need to live".
I stopped and waited for Love's reply
and the words came as a whisper.
"You have the answer for all others but none for
yourself. Read your heart, then come to me"
The mist faded into the blue and I stood and
the words surrounded me and I was alone.

ARE YOU LIVING?

Are you living the dream?
The dream that's living in your heart
or are you just waiting for your life to start?

*

Lonely is having a hand to hold but not
feeling the comfort

*

The day of happiness has come for
all
For everything is right with the world
and your world swirls around you.

SING

Sing, oh living song of hell, with the songs That
everyone will follow. Sing a tune that will make
the people sing and dance without tomorrow.
I too can hear the song and dance in the
misty light. I know the tune well for I swirl
and sway and move with the human tide.
I know the tune for it lives within my heart and soul.

I know the words are played on the harps of
greed. But yet we dance and sing its words.
My eyes are close to the end.
The end that I know will be the last
dying breath of humanity.

SOME ONE

Someone said silence is golden. I have silence. With it comes loneliness. Silence is golden only when you have someone to share it with.

WALK-IN A DREAM

Today comes with the rising sun and you
no longer fear tomorrow. For the days that
lie before you are the dream you dreamed
yesterday. Dreams are just dreams that will
lie in your heart until you make them come true.

If your yesterday has closed your eyes
to tomorrow, then lie down and sleep
through the life that might have been.

Speaking of tomorrow does not make
them come true but action is its birth.
Uncover your eyes and take control of
your dreams and live and enjoy.
For what is tomorrow but an unborn dream,
a dream you have not walked in, a dream
that is full of expectations truth, and love.

Walk in your dreams, mold it and
live it with all your heart.

ANOTHER DAY

Another day has ended, I have not
given, nor have I taken except for time.
The world is not a better place because
I have lived. The somedays and dreams
have grown dimmer and my heart
is heavy. I no longer walk my own
way, but follow the path of least
resistance. For I have closed my
mind and my eyes to what is around
me. I only hope that I leave this world
with as much love and happiness
as I have taken. I want to stop running
and face myself, but I am afraid of
what I'll see. How bright the rays of
the sun even when it's hidden behind
a cloud. So should the rays of your
hope, although they are covered by
your despair hope is your sunshine,
although it is covered for a time
the rays of your hope will shine.

IT WILL TAKE

It will take you many more years to
find out what you have done right,

It takes two seconds to
find out what you have done wrong.

YESTERDAY, WORD

Yesterday is a word that I have looked on as my youth and I loved it with all the passion of living. Tomorrow was a word that I feared. Growing up was a word I did not understand when it was revealed to me that tomorrow was my life. I was awaken as if the bright sun had fallen on my eyes. I was awakened but still not sure, of the word tomorrow. I trod softly on the breeze that called to me and held to the past but not as if it were my life. Then the soft voice of my tomorrows called to me and I held out my hand to the emptiness still not sure of the soft voice that was calling. For its brightness blind my eyes and I could not see. Yesterday called in a louder voice, beckoned me to stay where you know your peace and happiness lies as a soft bed. My eyes now wide open, I fly from yesterday's grasp and move to find my peace in my tomorrows before they turn into my yesterdays. Now my tomorrows calls in a louder voice and I follow.

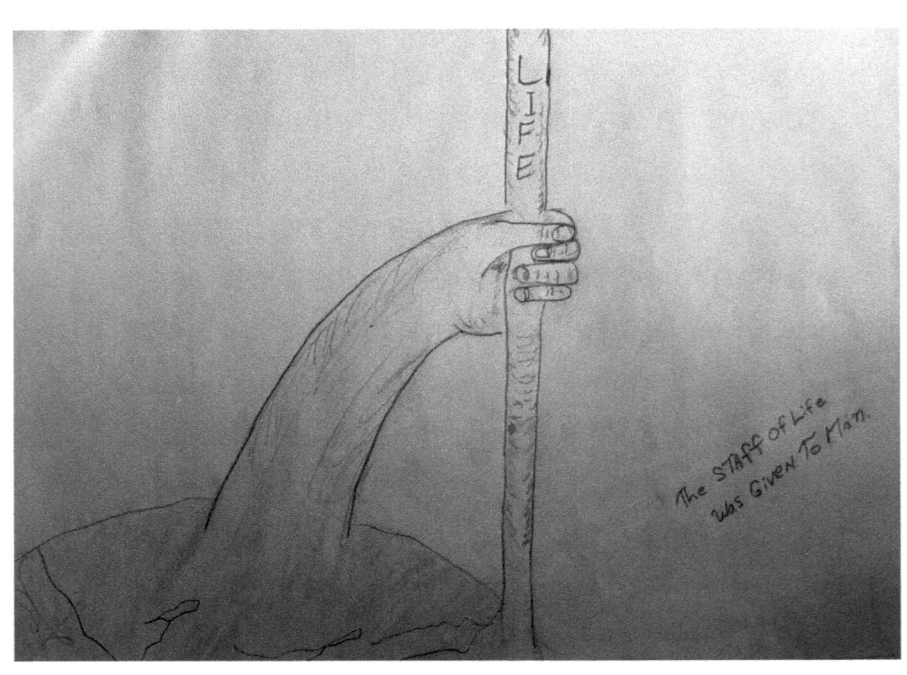

STAFF OF LIFE WAS GIVEN TO MAN

I HAVE LIVED

    I have lived life in
    dreams,
       grandeur,
          misnomers,
             fantasies.
all through my life has been true I have lived seeking.
I have spent my moment in time on earth
to share. I have shared. I do not regret my
moments in time, I have enjoyed them.
I would not turn back the hands of time
nor redo any part of my moments.
I have loved in many ways, and my truth has
been known. I do not doubt the truth that I have
known. Although at this moment I cannot see the
truth that is about me, it lies in front of my eye
for all to see but first, I need to know my truth.

I WANDER

I wander behind a cloudy haze,
knocking on door after door,
trying to get the answers to love,
hate and war I have a list of questions
   as far as you can see. Do you
   have any answer for me?
Why are there more words for sorrow than joy?
Why can't I stay a little boy?
Why is it cold when I want sun?
Why aren't sad thing fun?
Why are the things that are good bad for me?
Why is a snowflake beautiful until it hits the
ground? Why is the sun round? Why do birds fly?
Why do people say good-bye? How am I?

IT MAY

The stream of life is over you, you are drowning
from the human flow you try to swim its too
hard to do the tide of life has cover you.
You cry out to become a part of your own
to many people you can not be alone.
The human wave punchs you up and then
down some times you feel you will drown.
With all the fight with in you, you try to blend
in if you do you know it is the beginning of the
end. You dream of freedom and life just to live.
Ever person has something unto their
own your thought are your alone.

WE'VE

We've all been caught, telling a lie. But how many times have you been caught telling the TRUTH.

A PENNYS WORTH OF SLEEP

A warm summer night a night not for
sleeping A night in lost dreams
A night of twilight unrest.
I Close my eyes fighting the heat a small breeze
plays a melody on the window screen.
The sky filled with moon light
sprinkles thru the clouds
dancing across the sky, star light shining then
forgotten in the darkness. The heat deepens a
lite breeze brushes the clouds into the emptiness
leaving the loneliness for me to bath in.
The black tide travels slowly to the outer edge
of midnight My mind searches for the dawn
but the darkness prevailed. Then a splash of
light release me and a cool breeze break my
bound and I get a penny worth of sleep

I HAVE LIVED

I have lived my life to live I have taken,
  and I have tried to give.
    Maybe I have given too much.
      Maybe I have taken more than my share
        I have been loved and I have loved in return
          however, if I could relive my life, would I
            live it the same.
              Yes, I would
                But how do you be 36?

WHY DO I

Why do I want to ride on the wind?
What does it hold for me.?
Why do I wish to ride on the wind? Will it set me free?
Will I soar like a bird?
And know the secret of flight. Or will I be
left here on earth to join in the fight.

BEEN AT WAR

I have been at war where men kill men,
where lives have gone before my eyes.
I have been at war, where the blood
of man runs over the ground.
I have been at war, and have died a little
with each life that has gone before the
gun and yet we give a gun to the young
                              to kill.

I have been at war, where man's life oozed from
their body, as they watch themselves die and they
cry out. I have been at war for the last time.
No more will I see the blood of man dampen
the soil they lie on, at last, the war for me is
over and now I go beyond to peace for today

                      I die.

I HAVE ENJOYED

I have enjoyed the things I have known.
I have loved the time that was mine to spend.
Sure I would like to have had more. But
I know it is not mine to say, I'll die and be
delivered to a place of light. They'll judge
me and I'll be sentenced to eternity.
They will not ask me where I want to go,
if they did, I wouldn't know, for I have not been
in either place, and I don't know what awaits.

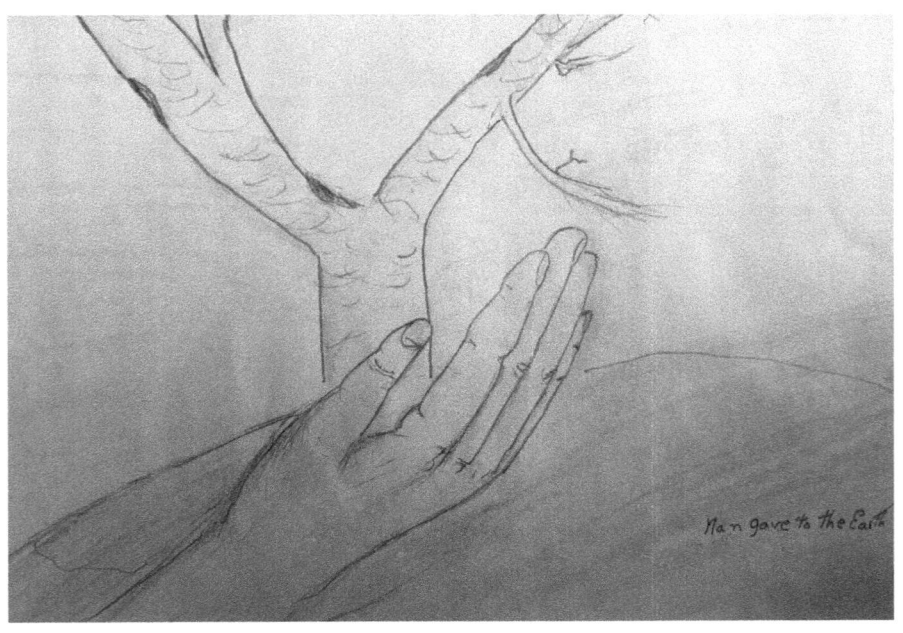

MAN GAVE TO THE EARTH

THE FUTURE

When I was young the future was today
I would kiss my mother and go
out and play. Twenty came and I thought
this is the future as it was meant to be.
So, I lived it as if it would never go away.
I took what I could and never looked
behind for to me the future was blind.
Fifty was here than sixty I still
didn't feel life slip away.

Seventy is here, now they say work is done.
Eight came and I looked at the future as
a scary place I think of my past as a soft
melody so I'll just live my song and be free.
I cry tears for the past
But only when I think of you I
cry tears for the past
For all the things we didn't have time to do.
But all the tears cannot make time redo.

*

I would kill myself
but I don't see any future in it

*

You know if tomorrow doesn't come I just die

HAND

I have called to people my storm of
life, and whispered my joy.
I have sung the tune of the land, and
played on the harp of death.
I have written poems for every
feeling I know and kissed the
mother of my child.
I have paid for and stolen time.
And now I hold out my hand.
It is spat upon,
chastised, and bleeding from the wounds.
I hold life firmly, for I know if I should let go,
I would slip into eternity
and be lost from this earth.

SUMMER NIGHT

The warmth of the summer lies heavy in stillness
no breeze to cool me. I lie still listening to the
silence Midnight comes and then becomes the
past. The darkness deepens and the pounding
of silence crashes into my brain.
Then in twilight sleep,
I travel. No light, but darkness surrounds me. I am
trapped in the darkness, and sleep devours me.
Now drifting in sleep, I am a prisoner of its grasp,
and it is midnight again. I do not rest. I fight my
way to the awareness from which I came.
When my eyes open to the light I see what the
darkness has not reviled, and life lives before me.

LISTEN

listen to the ticking of the
    clock, taken my life
    from me.
I watch the hands of
    the clock steal
    my living.
and I give to time so willing

SUCCESS

SUCCESS GROWS
 ON THE TREE OF EXPERIENCE
  SUCCESS IS ONE FRUIT OF
   LIFE WHEN PICKED IT WILL GROW

WORDS NO LONGER

Words no longer come to me in voice and rhythm.
My thoughts drift as a breeze on the
ocean and I am lost in time.
I am standing still and I know my
fate is old age. Oh, death,
I fight very little now.
I am content in my way of life,
and my song of joy is much sadder now.

My youth drained from me,
and I dream less of my dreams of life.
The sunshine in my tomorrows is not as
bright, nor do I squint my eyes to see.
For life has been good to me I will miss my life
But I will go quietly.

THE MELODY

The melody of motion floats on silver wings
and kisses the hand of eternity.
The golden voice of dreams,
calls to beauty unseen they singing
in your heart as it floats
across a sky clear and Blue.

THE TREE/YOUR YESTERDAY/I DON'T

The tree is straight and tall
                      But so is the weed

*

Your yesterdays are your path to your
today choose wisely or your tomorrows
                    will be hell

*

I don't weep for what I was yesterday
but for what I could have been.

DISSIDENT

Descent plagues our life and land.
The common, people don't understand to the old,
Descent is just a word it's a word
they have only heard.
The common folk just want to live.
They love the life they share.
To them, pollution is just something in the air.
The sky is blue enough to see.
The water is clean enough to be.
For the way they are, they will always stay,
Even if the blood should flow today.
No change No change.
Life, the same
Don't see, don't see I will live just for
me. Blacken the hills, kill far away.
But don't touch my life this day.
I have given to the cross of red,
   don't take my daily bread.
All the brutal thing you say, go from
    my life. I will not listen today.

GOOD BYE

Goodbye is a very long word and its loneliness can break your heart.

I CALL OUT

I cry Out, but only hear my words as an echo. I
look, but I only see my reflection and I cry.
I count my finger and toes they are the same.

I see my dreams are they the same?
I feel in this world of people I am one.

But where do go? Where do I belong?
How long can I search and not find?
How long can I cry and not know?

I reach out to the world, but it moves from me.
Can I go on without knowing, Is this my destiny?

NO LONGER

No longer does my mind and heart work
as one. For Love has forsaken me.
How lonely my loneliness how deep my
darkness when I am without Love.
My pride is no longer a comfort to me.

LOVE/BEAUTY/WHEN

Love Is

Love is like a pill
if taken with the right amount of water
It goes down easy Otherwise it hard to swallow

*

Beauty is within our soul
all we need do is
      open our heart and set it free

*

If your heart is full of love
      there is no room for heat

*

When your life is over
    your story is still untold.
        For it will be sung from the lips
      of those that love you

LOVE WAS YOUNG

When love was young and
words where soft dreams were
born in lovers' heart
Long gazes and lips that quivered
Lives were planned and young love starts.
When love was young
and hand that trembled, promise
was made for ever more.
In soft voices that would speak of
days to come and life to live and
hearts as one,
Life was simple and young eyes
would shine, when love was young
Life would fly on wings of a dove and
the two were very much in love.
Love grows old and
courses change but the
dreams are still the same.
Now life in silent bliss all words can
be spoken in a simple kiss.
Now no matter here or up
above the two were very
much in love and will stay
where love is young.

I AM NOT

        I am Not the first to
        lose something he has had my tears
        are not the first to fall Wonder-lust
        I didn't invent the
        word but I feel the last to fall

HALLELUJAH

Hallelujah the morning has come and gave
me a brand-new day Hallelujah the morning
has come and the lord said I may stay.
The Lord told me that this day was just meant
for me, with the bright blue sky and the green
grass and a hand to guide me on my way.
Hallelujah it is here, the brightest day I have
ever seen with crisp fresh air, the beauty of
spring with a new life that will grow everything.
The Lord has given me a smile on
my face a dream in my heart and a
chance for a brand new start.
I thank the Lord that he has given me the
gift of life and happiness, with ears to hear,
eyes to see, and the greatest gift of all.
The gift to love and to be loved,
the gift of understanding and faith
may I always live in harmony.

BLACKEST NIGHT

The blackest nights
Is before us.

They grow in darkness without
an end to be
The blackness holds us
and will not allow us to be free

Our blackest night lets hell
take our soul
heaven help us for God's sake.

Time has been given,

and taken from us too.
Our blackest nights are here
now it's how to live them through

TOMORROW

Tomorrow calls my heart to
sing another day.
I am filled with life
once more.
I have cried my
yesterdays and buried
them away.
Now I walk in the light of
today and search my heart
for the warmth of tomorrow.
The face of tomorrow has called
my dreams, and recalled my desires,
she held them in front of me.
But when I walk that way
she dances into another day.

GIVEN LIFE

I have been given life
and have followed its path.
I have taken life, with no words to
ask. I have floated on white fluffy
clouds, and let my mind travel
to faraway lands.

I have loved the things that nature

has grown, and I have let my
feeling be knowing.
Now with life half gone,
I find it hard to look beyond.
With eyes of youth and heart of age, the
Horizon dances in front of me.

What in life is there to give,
   I will Live,
      I will live.
         I will live.

OH

Oh, what a glorious day for you to see,
It is made for you and me. How can you
possibly explain to a blind man, what is
there? The beauty of the earth, the bright,
bright sun, and the clear blue sky.
Look up and see the sky is enough to take your
breath away. How do you tell a man that cannot see
the beauty of the mountains and the deep blue sea.
All the things that man walks by a blind
man would, give his life to see and die.
why does man's buildings reach the sky?
Can't, he see it from where they lie?
Stop and look at what I have found
A fresh new day.
Take a minute to look around,
I know that you will agree
that this is the way it is meant to be.

I HAVE NOTHING

I have nothing to cry for.
I have nothing to live or to die for.

I feel empty and dammed.
I am without words, song,
or beauty to see,

The only thing I could give to this life is me.
I stand in line awaiting life's call.

For emptiness has been
my food and I live.
For my food is plenty.

HOLY

When the sun brunches away the darkness
it awakes those that sleep and they
sing the song of the morning and
welcome a new day.

Their song of hallelujah brings all
the animals of the earth a bird
of the sky to rejoice the warming of the
sun and the rebirth of life.

WHEN I WAS YOUNG

When I was young, I would run to and fro
running just as fast as I could go I would
run up and down looking for something
I never Found. Now that I am old,
I walk where I go.

I am not fast nor am I slow because I
know where to go I don't have to
look up and down Because I
love what I have found.

THE WIND

I was a storm for a time, blown by the wind
traveling where the wind would take me.

Knowing no peace nor giving none.
Sometimes the wind would blow cold
   I could only stay for a moment in that life. The
   wind would come and pull me to another Place.
   Now the wind is still and the clouds
   are gone and the sun warms me.
   How calm the living without the wind.

*

MIDNIGHT MOON

Here I set under midnight moon
waiting for the dawn.

The dawn that will bring brightness to all that
welcome its warmth and to the ones that have
wondered in the darkness may they see the light.

BECAUSE

Because I live in dreams at times,
I make people madder than most.
I can see now why
Because when I live in dreams
I am gladder than most.
Why can't life and dreams be the same,
Do they differ only in name?
I have spoken in my dreams of life,
and I have heard.
But I cannot remember the words.

TO ALL SECRETS WILL COME A REVEALING

TOMORROW/FOR LIFE/PEACE

Tomorrow is not my
doom but my
Forgiveness
And the happiness
that dwells within my soul

*

For life has been
good to me
I will miss my life
But I will go quietly

*

Peace of mind
  is accepting yourself
    No matter how long it takes

A WHITE HORSE

Once I rode a white horse
down life path, I rode with
a wide smile on my face,
and a dream in my heart.

When all at once death took a
swipe at me and drove a spear
of pain into my heart. He took
me down to the cold hard
ground, I fought for my life
and won. Death took from
me my strength, dashed my
confidence to the ground
then slice my sense of will
bring to the bone. Now with
ever pitch, pain or ache
I think he has come for
me again. Even though death
has taken a swipe at me and
missed, the scar from his blade
will be with me until he wins.

THEY

They asked me
where I have been and
I replied
I was out groping in the darkness
searching for a
    tomorrow filled
    with light

I WONDER

wonder if the feeling
    I feel is me, or just
    what I want to be.
I dream the way I would
    like to be,
but if I were there,
would it really be me?
    I can put myself in that
place, and out again at
    will.
But to do and stay that
    way would I have
    the will?

THE FESTIVAL OF NOT RETURNING

I walk in darkness without light to see.
Now I am lost and walk without the purpose of life.
I walk without dreams. Or love.
                         I walk alone.
A hand to hold
   A footstep to follow A dream to cling to.
     A flower
       A clear blue sky,
                A wish to dream,
                   To Die
A promise of tomorrow, a forgotten yesterday.
Words are spoken, in a dream, I cannot remember.
For today is now and I walk alone.
Tomorrow is yet to come, and yesterday is
gone,not to be found in tomorrow's dream.
For today I walk and now I can see.

CHILDREN OF GREED

To you children of greed who count your life in Gold.
Who speak of only the things you have sold.
To get and keep reaping but never willing to sow.
Children of greed how can you be so bold to
gather unto you all the things that you think you
are due and you want no one to ask of you.
Can't you see after you are gone there
will be nothing left for the young.
Do you want your young to live?
If so, you'll have to start to give.
You'll have to put your gold aside
and think of others' lives.

LIKE I AM

Like I am you will never be,
for you have been and now it's
hard for you to remember
when.
Although we think a
part let me live with all my heart.
Let me see the world as new
not old like you.
Let me do things
you didn't do
Let me live my life for me not you.

I KNOW/THE SUN/SOMEONE

I know I am going to
die all want to know is
    When and why

    *

The sun and
moon Have
never met but
they shine from
the same light

    *

Someone ask me what is the
best thing that ever happen
to me.
I replayed
"My Birth without that you
wouldn't be asking me that
question"

I AM

      I am not the master of my soul
           nor of my being
      Something dwells with in me
           Calling out
   for my
   destruction
        And I run
        to its calling

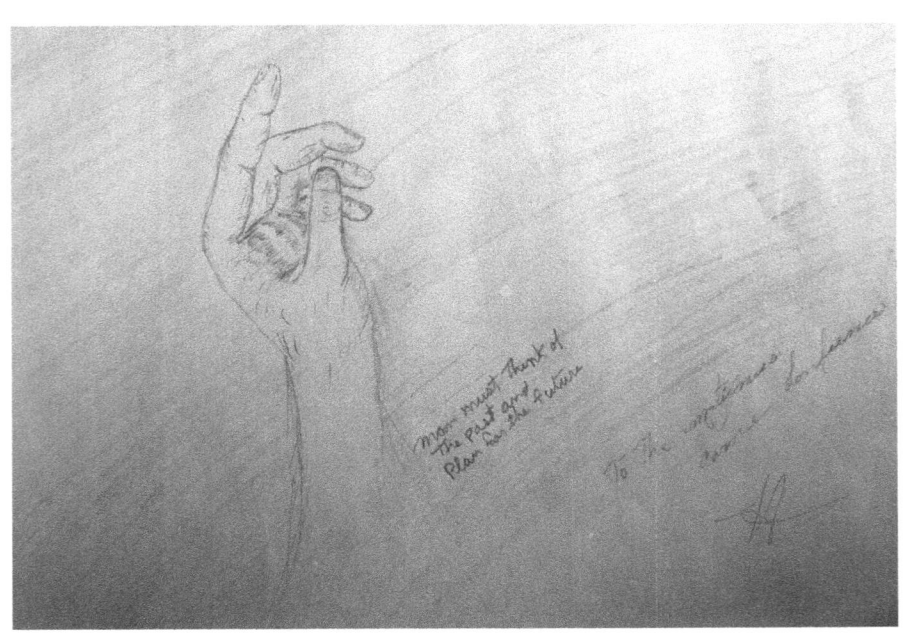

MAN MUST THINK OF THE PAST AND PLAN FOR THE FUTURE

LOVE SPOKE TO ME

Love came to me and spoke
"Tell me who I am" I thought for a time
before I spoke, I turned away. "Love"
I began "You are a dream You are
a thought You are a feeling a fantasy.
I stopped and turned to love but love
turn its back to me I tried to say more
but the words froze to my lips.
Love then spoke
"Until you know my truth,I
will walk from you"
I cried out
"I do know your truth"!
Love stopped but did not turn to me
          "Love" I began
"You are what all people need to live.
I stopped waiting for loves reply and
then Words came from the missed
"You have the answer for everyone
but yourself read your heart and
when you know your truth come
to me with an open heart.

HOW SWEET

How sweet life is when it is sung, in your key

IF I WERE YOUNG

If only I were young to see what I may see.
If only I were young to be what I may be.
If only I were young so I could measure time.
If only I were young to make my life rhyme.
The young men will soon be old and their ideas
not so bold. If all is well in not too many years,
the words of discord will reach their ears. It is
now, that they want what they think is theirs. But
tomorrow what was once theirs will be gone, and
it will be their yesterdays. So, take what
you will, drink from the cup but remember
there will be no one to fill it up.
Eat your fill, but if you look into tomorrow,
it will be still. I was young once and I ran,
hollered, and cried I leave you these words.
Love but don't eat mankind don't
take what can't be replaced.
Love all mankind, do not devour the human race.

BEFORE TODAY

      Before today is dead
      And tomorrow raises its head
      I want to stop
      And dream of yesterday

I HAVE COME

I have come this far without knowing,
but I have asked.
I guess the only time you get the answer to
life is when you don't need it anymore.

I FORECAST

I forecast infatuation tomorrow,
Love the flowing day
and drought the rest of your life.

MY PAST

My past is afloat on a white cloud.
Its bed is a dream.
It's pillow the warm sunshine.
It lies in my yesterdays as a soft
feather, floating in a clear blue sky.
I hold it with love in my heart
and I want to lie beside it in
times of peace.
Before I die

MAN IS

Man is but a moment
in life What of his
death

HOW DO YOU

How do you tell how old someone is?
Are you old because you are used and bent?
How do you tell someone age?
   are they counted in
      Tears,
         Pain
           or joy?
How do you number someone's years?
   By the steps,
   they have taken,
   either forward or back?
Are you young because it's years you lack?

THE WORDS

The words I write have been said, before
today I feel they mean even more.
Imagine, if you will, when you awake, you
are something different than before.
Imagine that you are a different color.
Would you be the same.?
Put yourself in a different race,and
see if you like that place.
Will people treat you as they did before, do
you like yourself less or more? Walk down the
street you walked, Go to the same people
and talk. Would it be the same?
would they know your name?

MY VOICE

My voice is silent my thought reaches
out to you for it is your voice
that I hear in my slumbers. It is your
voice that my heart hears.
My mind does not rule my heart it is my heart that is
the master. Should the last of the sunshine, or the
moon fall from its place in the sky, I could wait in the
depths of satins den, that I may just see your eyes..
No other love was born in my heart that it may seek
in a loud voice. No love would I want that *it* may blind
me. Your love is not as the chain of man prison, but
as the breeze that would carry the scent of roses.
If my years should out number all, if I should stand
alone on this earth, I would cry out your name.
That I may hear the sound of softness.

GOOD MORNING LIFE

Good morning life

what memories do you have for me today?
Are they happy or sad? Will I love them
or want them to go away?

Good morning life

Are your arms open to me? Will you

hold me or set me free? Can you give

me more time, to find my way?

or soon will the sun leave my

days? Good morning, Life!

Thank you for the morning dawn. And

for life itself, may it go on, and on.

I AM

I am a lonely man.

But not alone.

MORE

More than words life should be More than words love must be All in sweet melody. When life shines from your eyes for all to see everyone will sing your song in harmony…

I KNOW

I know the lies and pain of passion.
Love, its broken dreams seem to shroud
my path in black remembrance.
To speak of love is easy, we say the
words, to obtain the joy of passion.
My heart now cries, with the pain of each
yesterday.
Love, I fear that you have forsaken
me. But I have forsaken love.

THE VOICE OF THE MOUNTAIN

The voice of the mountain sings to me from afar,
calling my name calling in a way for me
to come to the place of dreams
    Peace
        freedom
            solitude

Where loneliness is forbidden
                where love is life,
spoken with the voice of yesterday.
The sweetness on your lips
    are one with love and love
    is one with you.
Contentment, beauty
The worth of life shines on you in a

way to make you what the next
    breath of fresh air and life
renewed in a soft melody.

FOR SHEEP

For sheep leap, and
clouds do fly.
Birds do sing, and so do I.
Although we are many
years from being one,
We have a common
ground. We have
fought and won.
It is this world we share.
It is this life we bear. We
must move as one.
We must save life, limb,

and breathing air. The
age of death is long, and
darkness for our eyes.
So, hear now all
living thing,we
are not here,
Just to die.

WORDS

    Words of today
        Words of the past
    Mean the same
        all we need to do is ask.

I LOOK

I look but do not see.
I touch but do no feel.
I listen but do not hear, the things,
that are good for me.
      I walk but go nowhere,
I talk but, the words
are not there
I think only of me.

AS FAR

As far as I can see, there isn't much left of me.
Spit out by the past and gobble up by today
'society. For there are songs they sing I do not
understand, or hear their melodies. I have lived
for many years and cried many tears. I have had
pain, sorrow, love, *joy, happiness, and hate*. Now
I feel empty as if I have walked on the outside
of a cool stream and not touched its waters.

There is a feeling I do not know and long for. There is
somewhere I have not been and dream of. There is
someone I do not know, and they await. My destiny
is an open book and I fear to turn the page. I fear the
darkness that is in my life I fear the open door, and
the cold that may shroud my mind, And I will freeze.

YESTERDAY

Yesterday has taken part of me, and
    today I must live.
Tomorrow stands and waits for me,
    and I know I will have to give.
With all the yesterday gone away,
I can face today.
Tomorrow will have to wait for me,
So, I may spend the time in front of me.

TOMORROW CALLED

My tomorrow called to me to follow. When
I was young, I would run to them, and the
faster I would run the future would run me.
Then I would slow, then the future would call in
A louder voice, "come to me, hurry, and
you will see".
    I would try to pick up the pace, but I would
    tire and all most stop.
"Come they would beacon."
"It will better when you reach here,"
I would pick up my body and push on,
    them time touched me.
No matter if I were to run or go at a slower
pace tomorrow would be there, and if they
were not, I would be in a better place.

I WAS A STORM

I once was a storm blown in the wind
traveling wherever the wind would take
me knowing no peace nor given none.
I would arrive in a life like a warm breeze
 not learning about them nor them about me.
Sometime the wind below cold and then
the wind would take me out of that place.
Now the wind is silent, and it is gone from
me.
The sun has warmed me and now I am at
rest.
How calm the living when the wind
does not blow

I HAVE SONG

I have sung my sorrows they
have been spent from me and I
fly on wings of happiness.
I have a song to sing that will
make you cry tears of joy.
For he that has never lived
in life let him live now.
Let him find the words in his
heart that will care him from
just living
        To Life and beyond.

TOMORROWS DREAM

I walk in a silent dream and as I run to my
yesterday's they stay in rhythm to time and move
as the wind. I was carried by the unforgiven tide
and cash into the unmovable shore. As the sea
I leap at the shore only to recede once more.
I leap once more as to break from my bonds,
and I leap into the unknown not to return. For
only the lifeless will time stands still. They stand
without motion waiting in timeless space for
the ticking of the clock to end a silent dream

LETTER TO A DREAM

I enjoyed your sweet and short
visit to my sleep you were very
welcome to my darkness
that encompassed me.
You added much to the
nothingness I was caught up in.
The fantasy you gave me made
my sleep worthwhile.
I know that you will not appear
in my bright sunshine
However, I will delight in your recall.
If time and space would ever
be the same, I welcome you
to steal me from the darkness
that comes each night.
It will bring to the emptiness joy
or pain, and I will enjoy the ride
on the wings of a dove or on the
sharp blade of your sword.
please come to me again.

Yours truly
    A sleeping mind

FOUR STROKES TO MIDNIGHT

Four strokes to midnight a bell tolls the final hour
a drink of wine hands claps in a final good-by

    A Kiss
        A Kiss

The sky reflects the flames of a burning city.
The mountain echo's the cries of the people
dying the city is empty and gone to dust life
is at an end for someone some were

    A Kiss
        A Kiss

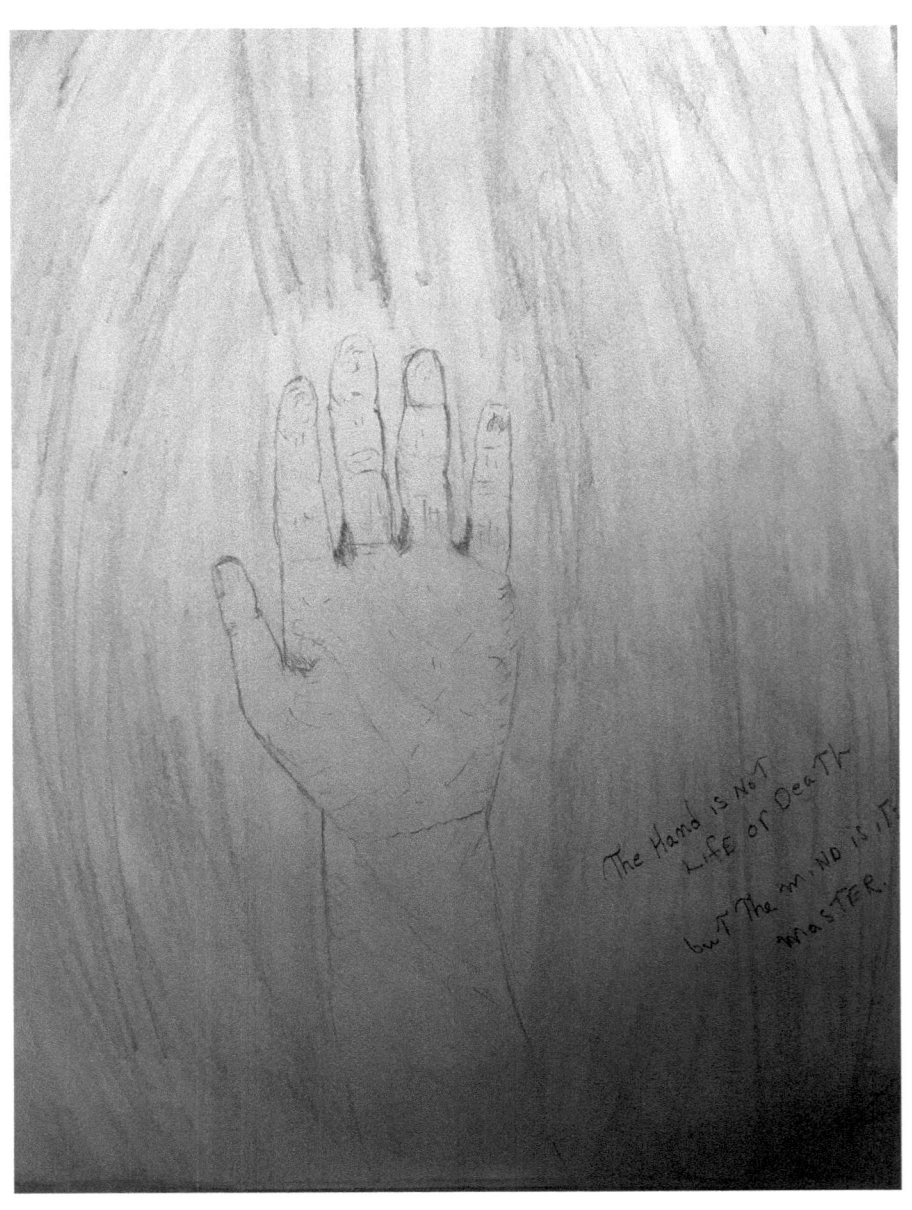

*THE HANDS IS NOT LIFE OR DEATH
BUT THE MIND IS ITS MASTER*

A TOP

A top a clod gray mountain Where
only the lonely dwell.
I stop for a time I felt the cold I feel the loneliness
I cry out my voice echoes in the emptiness.
I huddle with in myself to shield
me from the cold. I want
to walk down the mountain to a
warm and happy place.
I know it is there for me, but I am afraid
Now my pride in no longer a comfort to me.

I AM FIRM

I am a firm believer that everything is given
 to you only to be taken away.

    Your Life

    Your Wife

And the money you made today

LOVE IS

Love is as the ocean.
There is more to it
then you can see.
You can float on it
or you can drown in it

*

I love the sweet morning silence,
When I can be alone with a fresh new me,
For every morning I awake I
felt the need to be free.

I HAVE WALKED

I have walked on this earth
screamed of hate
Whispered of love
   I have asked and received
     I have been asked and
        have given
I have done these things to
find who I am, but my face
is hidden in the darkness

ONE THING

One thing I know for sure
   Love is like
      water
if it flows it will stay fresh

but if it stands still,
it will grow stale
and draw bug

SING OH HEART

Sing oh heart that I may live this
day in happiness. Sing oh heart
as you did when I was young.
Give me the glory that I may see
life's sweet melody to see the day
through the eyes of my youth.
Let my heartbeat within my
chest as if I had a new love,
give me the strength to live
and take life as it is given.
I now know the power of life and its
joy, and I give thanks for it every day

*

It easy to find LOVE however to keep it you need
Trust, understanding, and Faith
It is more fun to make memory's
then to remember them.

THERE IS

There are only two things on this earth that
I am frightened of

LIFE
and
DEATH

*

I know not why I write words upon a page.
I write when I am happy,
I write when I am sad
But I am happy not sad that I do.

IN TIME OF PEACE MAN IS ONE

ACKNOWLEDGE

Acknowledge the past and throw
it away hold close to you, your
todays or the darkness will take
it from you.
Rejoice in your tomorrows for
they are the past not lived
remember if your tomorrows come
too soon they will be eaten by your
yesterdays before you can live them.

TODAY

Today is mine to have all its love and
pain today I must take
for it will not be given again.

THEY SAY/ IF YOU

    They say that age is just a state of mind
        the only thing my body is in another state

        *

    If you put as much thought in to telling the truth
        as you do telling a lie
            You would always tell the truth

WAS IT THE MASTER?

Was it the master from his place in the world?
Who said?
"Bring me your needs and
I shall show you the path to your desires."

"Bring me the pain in your heart and
I will show you the mirror that
you may see your truth".
Was it not the master that has named
every feeling? was it the heart and soul
of the master that came to us in our
hours of need holding out this hand to
help us cross the bridge to life.
But wasn't it us that with heart and
soul gave him our hand?

IT'S COME UP AGAIN

It's came up again, my past as I know *it to be.*

My fears, and what it's going to be.
My Mind Is a blaze with all the
thought that could be but I cannot
catch one and hold it to me.
My thoughts frolic like the wind in
some lofty tree.
They push and pull at me.
I search for the place I want to be.
But like the wind,
I guess there will be no rest for me.

WALK IN LIFE

To you that walk in a lie and call man God.
To you who believe not in a god I say to
you, you have died and you walk in life as a
cloud blown in the wind you did not see
your begging. I say to you
You will see your ending and you will
live it with frightening awareness

You're beginning and ending has been written.
Even the suns path has been writen.

Even the passing of time has been written
as the number of the stars in heaven is
unknown your ending is unknown.
Even as you read these words and believe or
disbelieve. You cannot remember your begging
nor will you remember you're ending.
As man does not remember the beginning of time
nor will he remember the last
minute of time on this earth.

I say unto you there has been a record that has
been written and you are marked in time.

ASK

Ask not more than your labors can give you,
take not more than you are due. Ask, only
that you receive true love and take not a
false one to you. Give only your true self
to the world. Keeps unto you your happiness
that will save your soul. See the truth in
people take their truth unto you.
Take their truth from them and save in your heart.
Hold unto you the happiness to come to you.
Cast out the sadness that they will service.
Draw from them the courage and hope to
replenish your courage and hope.
Do not drain from them all that they
have, and leave them empty.
For your walk is the one that will carry

You to your goals It is your breath
that will make your heartbeat.
Your heart is the one that will spin
your love into the clear blue sky.

SILENT

How silent a beautiful dream. How sweet it seems.
A dream for one path to walk, Words in silent talk
A beautiful dream where winds do not blow
where your love can rest for a time.
How silent a beautiful dream where warmth
holds you without the cold or rain.
Oh, silent dream let me live within you, let me
hold you let me hold you even in my awareness
let me escape the wind and the cold
let me live with a happy heart unit I grow old.

HAVE

I have followed the darkness
and kissed the light.
I have followed love living
as I might.
I have given all I had to give,
I have lived and let live.
I have walked alone in
silkie white, to live in the
brightness of the light.
I dream the dream of
yesterday, seeking the
love of today.
For now, that I have lived
this day,and given it to time,
I wander in the sky of
blue seeking that which
is in my mind.

THE WIND

The wind whispered to me to sleep,
then the thunder came and I slipped into
the darkness of the night and it
called my sleep from me.
My thoughts came to me in my
awareness and the silence of the
darkness pound loudly in my brain
and sleep, slipped from me again.

   When will I find sleep, Is it in the early
   dawn? Will slumber pursue me in the bright
   of the day. Where will I find sleep.?
   Will my slumbers follow me into the night?
   and let the dreams flow or will I stay
   awake and watch my dreams go

MORE THAN / I WAS NEVER

More than death life should be or is life going to
be the death of me. More than today. Yesterday
is mine for I have locked it away in my memory to
have when I am lonely. More than today tomorrow
is mine for, I have locked it away in my dreams.
More than yesterday or tomorrow
is mine for now, my dreams
can come true.
For I feel the glow of life by the living I do.

*

    I was never in a hurry to
        grow up now
       I know why

I NO LONGER

I no longer run with time
But Walk with its grasp
and listen to its
Melodious song

I AM HERE

I am here because an urgent melody
beckons me. I am here because this dark
and lonely place has called me.
    I have come on the dark wings of loneliness.
    I have come although I did not know what
    awaits me.
I can see now why I have come. For I
have no yesterday to return to
Now the urgent melody calls me
a bright new tomorrow.
Happiness floats around me and the
brightness of thousand days to come.

YESTERDAY

Yesterday was the time for tears.
Today is new and here to live.
Tomorrow is yet to come

for life is growing with in you
the sky is not far away so grab
your wings and fly.

*FROM THE MYSTERY OF LIFE COMES
THE HANDS OF THE MIND*

IN ALL

In all the days of man's world
    Let there be, the light of tomorrow

WITH LOVE

Tomorrow can be more than a dream

TO MY FATHER 1984

We weep to see you have gone from our living
we tremble at the sight of your castle with out
light we hold one another and ask for our peace.
Your peace has been given to you walk in that
peace it is not a peace we can understand
your hands are cold but your soul warms us
as it dances across the sea of eternity.
You are going to a place were peace
is king and love abounds.
Our tears are not going to hasten your return
but they are comfort to our soul, we send
you off with our love to keep you warm .
You may not be in our living but you
will never be out of our lives.

I AWOKE

I just awoke from a dream.
A dream that Left me in despair
I was on a planet called earth,
and confusion reigned there.
There were people of all kinds,
shapes, and colors and they
called each other brothers
but they fought and killed each other.
There were cries for peace,
but all you could see is their
tears from their crying.
No one was willing to give,
or ask for help from above.
The planet was the richest in the
universe, but the multitudes
were hungry for peace and they
cried in pain.
The few that had were not willing
to give or to look at how the multitude
lived.

I'LL CRY/LIFE IS/LOVE HATE

I'll cry tomorrow with tears
of yesterday for things, I have today.
For life is mine and glows with in me
And I am blessed to wake up and see a new day

*

Life is a blessing Death is a curse
some time I
wonder which
one is the worse

*

Being selfish is not sharing the day when it is perfect

*

Love
>This word is as mystical as the
moon as distant as the stars
and as vast as the universe

Hate
>can be as deep as the ocean as hot the sun
and as destructive as an earthquake

I HAVE BEEN LISTENING

I have been listening to both to the old and the new.
They both think they have the answer and They Do
    and
        They Do
Each person can add something to what could
be done but no one is listing to any one
they are thinking of just one.
You can say all you want to about people
    their Hate,
        Loves
            and
                Wars
You can say all you want about people
but people are not people any more.
They walk down the street and pass one another
if one falls down, they will step on their brother.
You get caught up in the race and you can't stop
running you got to keep pace with the society that
is drumming. You think to yourself how to get out
of this place but there is only one human race.
You get caught up in a world of people
you feel dark and alone and you fear that
someday you will be looking for a home.
I see people racing by to hear and there
and I wonder if they know too were.

HAPPINESS/I SPEND/IT IS/SOME

Happiness is having lips to kiss
and understanding why

*

I spend my live-in bliss now that the light
of My life warms the spirit of my soul

*

It is WE that makes our light shine
It is I light that blind us

*

Some say all you have to do is to
love That's the easy part

THE BREATH

>The breath of life
>>flows as wine
>And I am bound to
>>drink all of mine

ACID RAIN

Feelings of others can fall on you like acid rain.
Let your faith be your umbrella

*

Faith and tomorrow mean the same

*

There is a thin line between love and hate
There is no line between Love

*

Your mind can tell a lie, but your heart can not

*

They say time marches on
But always feel I am out of step

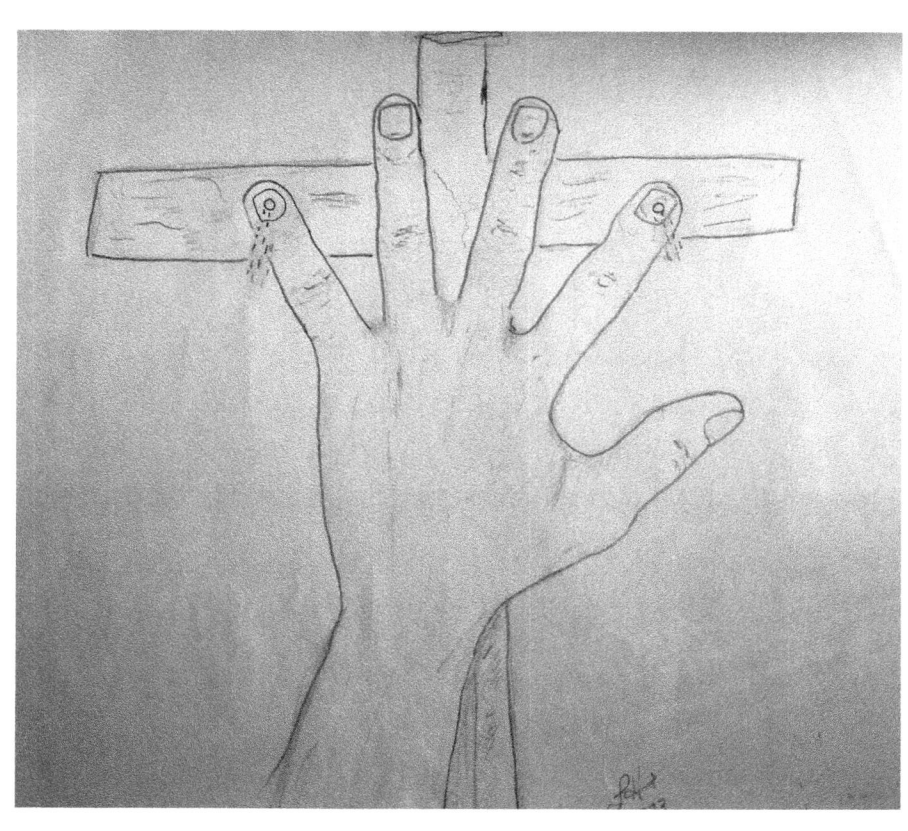

AT THE END

At the end of all, there is,can there be any
more? After the door is closed, is that all there
is for sure? When the water recedes, will it
always return to the shore? or, after the tide
is gone, will it never return anymore.?
When the wind ceases to blow and everything is still,
Will this be the end of the Grass waving on the hill?
When the sun fails to rise, will darkness prevail?
When the moon ceases to appear,
Is the end very near?
When all the things that we have that
are good have gone by the way,
Can we live in that world today?

www.ingramcontent.com/pod-product-compliance
Lightning Source LLC
LaVergne TN
LVHW051225070526
838200LV00057B/4605